1.1
Risk identification and management

Course Book Chapter 1

Internal, external or mixed provision

Course Book Chapter 2

- Public, private, third sector providers
- Relevant policy
- Governance arrangements

1.0
Business case for contracts

1.3
Approval and authorisation to proceed

Course Book Chapter 3

- Approval levels
- Approval procedures for projects
- Stakeholder consultation

1.4
Involving procurement staff

Course Book Chapter 4

- Importance of early involvement
- Procurement knowledge/competencies
- Communicating skills

1.5
Appropriate funding mechanisms

Course Book Chapter 5

- Whole-life costing
- Investment appraisal techniques

Risk is 'the probability of an unwanted outcome happening' *(CIPS):* a combination of the **probability** of an event (the likeliness of its happening) and any foreseeable adverse **consequences** or outcomes arising from it.

Sources of risk impacting on procurement decisions

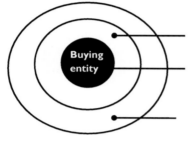

Micro (industry) environment:
Competitors, customers, suppliers etc: industry structure; supply market factors
Porter's Five Forces Model: >> Unit 2.1

Internal environment:
Policies and procedures; security/controls; ethics; skills; technology; management etc

Macro environment:
PESTLE factors in wider external environment: 'uncontrollables'

Macro (external) environment risk: the PESTLE model

Factor	Examples of sources of risk
Political	Changes in government policy; tax and employment law; foreign trade regulations; political instability, terrorism or social unrest in markets
Economic	Business cycles (eg recession); interest/foreign exchange rates; inflation; employment; infrastructure development in markets
Socio-cultural	Changing demographics (gender roles, age distribution, population growth); cultural values and norms; education and skilling
Technological	Technological change and obsolescence; cost/risk of innovation; challenges of virtual organisation; data security risks
Legal	Changing compliance risks from national/EU requirements (eg on health & safety, environmental protection, public sector procurement)
Environmental	Compliance risks of legislation (eg on pollution, waste, GHG emissions); scarcity/cost of natural resources; impact of weather and natural forces

Using PESTLE analysis	
☑ Simple, inexpensive	☒ Oversimplification
☑ Overview of macro environment	☒ Difficult to anticipate future factors
☑ Encourages strategic thinking	☒ Too much data > analysis paralysis
☑ Supports identification/management of threats and opportunities	☒ Poor quality data, based on assumptions or pre-identified issues

Types of risk

Political risk	Change in government policy, priorities or project plans Political imperatives or national emergencies by-pass VFM principles
Limited competition in market	Specialist requirements > may be few available/quality suppliers: - Risk of exploitation by suppliers in strong bargaining position - Risk of exposure/loss as a result of supplier failure
Failure to meet standards	Risk of suppliers failing to meet performance standards. Due to: poor specification; lack of supplier pre-qualification/appraisal; lack of performance management and problem resolution mechanisms
Change of law	UK and EU law impacts on procurement processes (eg public sector procurement directives) and requirements (eg re product safety, energy efficiency, use of hazardous materials, recyclability)
Security of supply	Risk of supply disruption, switching costs. Depends on: no. of suppliers in market; availability of supply; supplier stability and risk management; single/multiple sourcing. Need for: contingency planning, buffer stocks, alternative sources for critical items.
Quality, project or technology failure	*Quality*: risk of operational disruption, reputational damage, safety/performance issues. Due to: poor quality management. *Project*: risk of schedule/cost over-run, failure, accidents etc. Due to poor specification, tight timescale, poor project management. *Technology*: risk of systems breakdown, loss/theft of data. Due to: poor maintenance, human error, sabotage, teething problems.
Supplier insolvency	Risk of disruption of supply, reputational damage. Due to: insufficient assets, poor management, economic/market conditions. Mitigated by: parent company guarantees or performance bonds; monitoring of supplier integrity, financial stability and capability.
Security, theft and damage	Risk of damage/theft in transit or in stock, and resulting loss/liability. Due to: inadequate security measures, poor storage/handling arrangements, inadequate insurance.
Fraud, conflict of interest and ethical risk	*Fraud*: deliberate deception (eg accounting/payment exposure: diversion of funds, falsification of data). *Conflicts of interest*: eg inducements to award contracts (corruption) *Ethical risk*: eg breach of confidentiality, integrity. Need for codes of purchasing ethics, conduct etc + internal controls
Contractual failure	Risk of supply failure, loss, legal dispute. Due to: poor contracting, lack of contract management. Loss arising from failure (*consequential loss*) may be mitigated via financial compensation stated in the contract (*liquidated damages*) or other remedies.

Procedures to manage risks

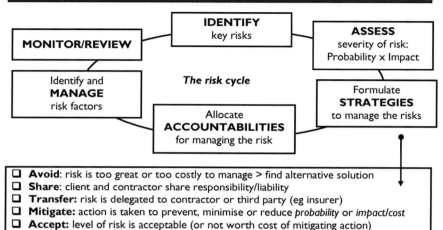

- ☐ **Avoid:** risk is too great or too costly to manage > find alternative solution
- ☐ **Share:** client and contractor share responsibility/liability
- ☐ **Transfer:** risk is delegated to contractor or third party (eg insurer)
- ☐ **Mitigate:** action is taken to prevent, minimise or reduce *probability* or *impact/cost*
- ☐ **Accept:** level of risk is acceptable (or not worth cost of mitigating action)

Allocation of risks between client and contractor	Share or transfer risk, according to which party is best placed to *manage* risk Client should retain risk where (a) in best position to manage risk, (b) exposure is minimal (compared to costs of sharing/transfer), or (c) insurance coverage is cost-effective
Risk register	List of identified risks for a unit, operational area or project: risk details, mitigation strategies, allocation of responsibilities etc.
Governance arrangements	*Contractual incentives and penalties:* eg specific KPIs and project milestones linked to payments under the contract
	Liquidated damages: provision for appropriate damages payable for non-performance, specified in the contract as a genuine estimate of consequential loss (*liquidated damages*).
	Relationships: contract and relationship management, ensuring that both parties understand and fulfil risk management responsibilities: contact mechanisms for reporting, review and problem handling
Risk monitoring	Monitoring registered risks on an ongoing basis: keep risk ratings up to date; ensure that mitigating strategies are operating etc. Reports, standing agenda items etc for: risk management group (evaluation of strategic risks), audit committee (evaluation of risk management process) and/or management board (general responsibility for risk management and operations).

CIPS Study Matters

Level 5

Advanced Diploma in Purchasing and Supply

PASSNOTES

Contracting in the Public Sector

© Profex Publishing Limited, 2010

Printed and distributed by the Chartered Institute of Purchasing & Supply

Easton House, Easton on the Hill, Stamford, Lincolnshire PE9 3NZ

Tel: +44 (0) 1780 756 777

Fax: +44 (0) 1780 751 610

Email: info@cips.org

Website: www.cips.org

First edition December 2009
Reprinted with minor amendments October 2010

Contents

Preface

Welcome to your **Passnotes**!

This element of your Study Pack has been specially designed to support you in your exam revision.

- Small-format **Passnotes** fit easily into a bag or briefcase: **convenient to use** wherever and whenever you have a few minutes for topic review or exam revision.

- The material is organised in **short, clearly labelled units**: easy to work through systematically or to dip into at any point, if that's what you prefer.

- Each area of the unit content starts with a simple **mind-map** of the relevant Learning Objectives, helpfully **cross-referenced** to chapters in your Course Book (so you can quickly locate more substantial topic coverage, if you need to refresh your memory).

- The units cover each (and all) of the **Learning Objectives** in turn (again, cross-referenced to other units where topics overlap), so you can see exactly what knowledge and understanding underpins potential exam questions.

- Within each unit, the material is presented in a format specially designed for **ease and speed of learning** – essential in the revision stage of your studies! **Passnotes** use key definitions, point lists, action plans, tables and diagrams:

  - To keep the topic coverage as focused and brief as possible
  - To offer an easily grasped overview of each topic
  - To make the topic more visual – and therefore (for most people) more readily memorable.

- For relevant topics, we also include Integrated Learning Checklists: point lists and action plans gathered from different Learning Objectives to give you a broader handle on topics, processes and management challenges. (Particularly useful for case study questions…)

Of course, Passnotes don't give you substantial or comprehensive coverage of the unit content. (That's what your **Course Book** is for.) What they do give you is **systematic and focused coverage**: a concise, easy-to-remember survey of the key points on which you can base an exam answer. This makes them ideal to use in the weeks and days leading up to the exam!

And don't forget: updates, case studies, advice on exam technique and other revision-support resources (including practice questions with full solutions) will be regularly added to the study resources.

Good luck.

Internal, external or mixed provision

 A **competition strategy** secures maximum benefits from procurement, using an evidence-based, transparent and auditable decision-making process.

Internal options	External options	Mixed options
☑ Retains skills ☑ Lower lifecycle costs ☑ Employee insight ☑ Retains control over resources. *But:* for Best Value, internal services must be exposed to 'genuine competitive pressure'.	**Market testing**: in-house provider bids in open competition v private or voluntary sector to identify best value provider. **Outsourcing**: contract awarded to best value external service provider, via competitive tender.	**Partnership** with another public, private or voluntary organisation to provide a service jointly, *or* to finance service provision by a third party. Not usually subject to tender: commercial negotiation or dialogue.

Business review:

☐ Is the service still required? If no, discontinue.

☐ Is service competitive? If no, consider internal/external/mixed improvement options

☐ Model costs/benefits of options over five years to identify best VFM and affordability.

Option	*Arguments for and against*
Cessation of service	☑ Little or no demand from 'customers' ☑ Costs of provision outweigh overall benefits ☑ Other (better or less expensive) providers exist ☒ Statutory duty to provide ☒ Evidence from business review is unclear/contradictory ☒ Only way of reaching a discrete/vulnerable group
Private Finance Initiative contract *External*	☑ Promotes change/development (constrained by public ownership) ☑ Allows delivery where legal/practical constraints on internal delivery ☑ Exploits private sector innovation, resources ☒ Not viable for small-value or urgent contracts ☒ Need to demonstrate VFM ☒ Need for service and continuous improvement KPIs, penalties etc
Outsource: transfer service to another provider (no in-house bid) *External*	☑ Solution to continuing/extensive internal failure/uncompetitiveness ☑ Suits new service area, where organisation lacks expertise ☑ Access to best provider, innovation, expertise etc ☑ Cost savings (from divestment, redeployment of resources) ☒ May be better options to address smaller service problems/issues ☒ Employee relations/TUPE issues ☒ Difficulty/cost of ensuring service/value/ethical standards ☒ Need to balance lifecycle benefits vs transactions costs, risks ('lock in' to potentially incompatible provider; loss of control; loss of in-house knowledge; loss of internal 'fall back' position)

Market testing of all or part of service *External*	☑ Robust test of perceived quality/cost of service ☑ Can tackle a specific area of service identified as needing change ☒ Market consultation may reveal lack of interest, or opposition ☒ Costly process, with uncertain outcome/benefits ☒ Not worthwhile if in-house provider has no chance of winning
Restructure/ reposition in-house service *Internal*	☑ Required where no developed supply markets for service ☑ Required where legal/practical/policy issues rule out competition ☒ Not viable where contracts do not allow for change/negotiation ☒ Not viable where costs of change outweigh benefits ☒ Not viable where contractor's performance is unacceptable
Joint delivery or financing/ commissioning of service *Mixed*	☑ Brings in expertise, innovation and additional resources ☑ Pooled resources may offer value, effectiveness, market impact ☑ Supports further improvement of positively-reviewed service ☑ May exploit shared mission/values (eg of third sector orgs) ☒ No benefit where organisation is already leader in the field ☒ Not viable where no suitable partners available ☒ Contracts may be too complex to cover eg regional variations
Setting up new unit to deliver service *Internal*	☑ Suitable where review has identified service gap, user need ☑ Suitable for taking over provision from existing body ☒ Cost of provision may be prohibitive ☒ Requires clear need identification, available budget
Call-off/term contracts etc *External*	☑ Allows flexible provision during periods of peak demand ☑ Performance benchmarks to improve existing service provision ☒ Not suitable for work of short duration, uncertain quantity
Involve trusts, charities, user groups etc *External*	☑ Supports community involvement and development ☑ Allows some accountability ☒ Not viable where services require regulation, technical expertise ☒ Better economies of scale available through other options

Strategic sourcing policies

Contracting out	Engage key stakeholders (incl. staff, management, trade unions) Specify service requirements as outcomes/outputs (not inputs) Consider use of incentive (contingency, bonus) payments Cost present activity as benchmark for evaluating proposals In-house bids treated same as outside bids in competitive tender Develop contract management skills
Competitive tendering	Best Value framework for service planning, delivery and improvement: Challenge, Comparison, Consultation, Competition Competitive tendering promotes fair competition, transparency, procurement efficiency EU public procurement directives: compulsory competitive tendering over expenditure thresholds *[>> Units 4.1 – 4.3]*

Use of private finance	Government commitment to efficiency, equity, accountability and public sector reform
	PFI only used if delivers clear VFM without sacrificing terms and conditions of public sector staff
	Over long term, PFI aimed to deliver quality public services/assets

Use of third sector expertise	Public services need to be flexible/responsive to customer concerns
	Voluntary & Community Sector offers: knowledge/skills for specialist services; citizen participation in service delivery; independence from existing models; cost-effectiveness of provision
	Framework for public/VCS partnership (1998)

Determining governance arrangements

How will internal/external/mixed provision decisions be made?

Transaction cost (Williamson)	Relational competence (Cox)
The decision of whether to make/do or buy depends on comparison of the transaction costs of each approach.	Core strategic competencies (value-adding, distinctive, non-replicable): need to maintain direct control > *internal* provision
Most important determinant of transaction cost is *asset specificity*: extent to which an asset's value depends on a particular relationship.	Complementary competencies: need to exploit efficiencies + maintain control > investment in collaboration or shared ownership
Specific assets > higher transaction costs > *internal* provision more efficient. Non-specific assets > *external* provision Medium specificity > *mixed* provision	Residual (non-critical, easily accessed) competences: low transaction/switching costs > competitive bidding to secure lowest-cost procurement

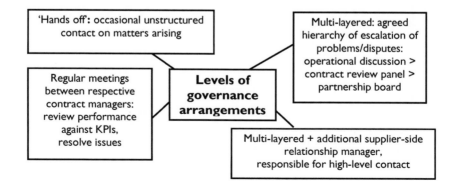

'Hands off': occasional unstructured contact on matters arising

Regular meetings between respective contract managers: review performance against KPIs, resolve issues

Levels of governance arrangements

Multi-layered: agreed hierarchy of escalation of problems/disputes: operational discussion > contract review panel > partnership board

Multi-layered + additional supplier-side relationship manager, responsible for high-level contact

Delegated authority for procurement

Authority should be clearly defined and delegated for budgets (and associated strategic and financial management responsibilities) and purchasing.

 A **Scheme of Delegation** details internal structures for the delegation of authority to senior executives across the organisation, and further sub-delegation as appropriate. **Accountable Officers** determine how authority should be delegated to individual managers.

❑ Info on levels of approval for purchase, and means of obtaining authority to proceed: 'Standing Orders', 'Finance Manuals' and 'Procurement Manuals'.

❑ General **levels of authorisation** for procurement:

Value		Category	Procedure	Authority
Low	<£1k	Goods/services/ works	1 verbal/ written quotation	Local officer
	<£5k	Goods/services	1 written quotation	Local officer
	<£10k	Works	1 written quotation	Local officer
Intermed.	£5k – £50k	Goods/services	3 written quotations	Section manager
	£10k – £50k	Works	3 written quotations	Section manager
High	£50k – EU threshold	Goods/services/ works	Sealed tender	Department head
	Over EU threshold	Goods/services/ works	EU tender exercise	Procurement unit

❑ Where three written quotations or tender are not possible, a nominated officer of suitable rank may authorise exception (with formally documented reasons).

❑ **Stages of contract approval** (contracts £5m+, Higher Education):

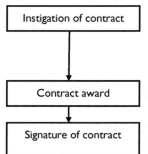

• Approval by Authority: Authority Resource Management Board review/approval of business case

• ARMB approval of budget availability

• Full formal tender (at least four tenderers)

Approval by Authority

• Director of Procurement Services (goods, services)
• Director of Estates (works, buildings)
• Director of HR (employment contracts)

Approval procedures for programmes and projects

 The OGC **Gateway Process** examines programmes and projects at key decision points, and authorises progress to the next stage if the review determines that this can be done successfully.

❑ Best practice in local govt, health and defence: mandatory in central civil govt.

❑ Based on 'peer reviews' by independent practitioners outside the programme: re progress, likelihood of successful delivery, project issues and challenges

❑ Provides assurance for authorisation at key decision points

 PRINCE2 is a UK government guide to the management of projects, designed for the public sector (and other 'controlled environments'). It provides a shared structure, process and terminology for stakeholders.

Authorisations within PRINCE2:

❑ **Project initiation**	Project Board authorises initiation. Project brief is developed > business case. Controls established.
❑ **Stage controls**	Overall project is broken down into stages. Each stage is controlled: authorising work, monitoring changes, taking corrective action on variances.
❑ **Managing delivery**	Ensuring each work 'package' accepted, executed and delivered to defined criteria.
❑ **Stage boundary management**	Ensuring smooth transition from one stage to next: delivery of all outputs, authorisation of next stage, approval of changes, documentation of learning

 Managing Successful Programmes (MSP) is a structured, flexible framework for managing and controlling programmes (co-ordinated projects).

Quality management	Risk management	Benefits management
Stakeholder management	**Governance arrangements in MSP**	Resource management
Issue resolution		Planning and control

☑ More effective delivery of change via integrated planning/implementation
☑ Improved focus on business objectives, business case and risk management
☑ Improved control: costs of new standards and quality regimes justified, measured
☑ Improved change management and transition via preparation, communication
☑ More efficient resource management: project prioritisation and integration
☑ Efficient co-ordination and control of complex activities: defined roles, benefits

Consultation with stakeholders

	Stakeholder	Interest (stake)	Influence/power
Internal	Managers/ employees	Survival/growth of employer Task/personal goals	Formal authority Control over resource/skills
Connected	Users/ Beneficiaries	Adequate services, safe products Ethical dealings	Power to boycott/switch Legal remedies
	Financers/ taxpayers	Accountability/transparency Value for money	Power to withhold funds Power as voters
	Suppliers & distributors	Reliable revenue stream Information/feedback support Mutually beneficial relationship	Control strategic resources Expertise (eg subcontractor) Strategy implementation
External	Interest groups	Awareness of cause/issues Protection of rights	Power to lobby, boycott, generate publicity
	Trade unions, prof. bodies	Protection of rights of members Promoting standards/ethics	Control over members Advisory/consultative
	Community/ wider society	Employment and amenities Provision of goods/services Social responsibility	Voters and taxpayers Target beneficiaries 'Owners' (via the State)

❑ Diverse stakeholder constituency >> focus on accountability, stakeholder consultation, defining stakeholder value

❑ Ethical and practical obligation to inform stakeholders re: new info, plans, decisions likely to affect their activities or interests; changes to data, plans or decisions likely to be relied upon

❑ Legal obligation to inform stakeholders eg re changes to contract terms; consultation of trade unions on issues affecting member interests

❑ Gathering info *from* stakeholders: eg market engagement; stakeholder feedback; joint definition of objectives, 'value', rights/obligations

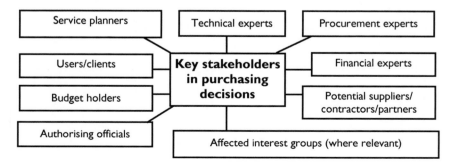

Evaluate the importance of involving procurement staff with expertise appropriate for the requirement at an early stage

1.4

Involving procurement staff... at an early stage

Early buyer involvement is a process whereby procurement staff are involved at an early stage in the product/service development process, making proactive suggestions to improve designs and materials specifications.

Advantages of involving procurement at an early stage	Risks of not involving procurement at an early stage
Ability to prioritise/rationalise purchases (eg consolidation, variety reduction)	Inadequate planning of the procurement process > inefficiency, failures
Ability to challenge client definitions of requirement > better value, sustainability	Poor specification, over-specification, unsustainable specification
Supply market awareness (potential suppliers, generic items available, technologies, risk factors etc)	Fraudulent activity by potential suppliers (without whole-life contract management)
Contacts to support early supplier involvement, partnership development	Compliance risk: breach of EU directives, Standing Orders or other regulations
Commercial/legal expertise for specification development	Poor procurement disciplines: overlooking OGC guidance
Purchasing disciplines > variety/cost reduction, value analysis etc.	Lack of commercial expertise: loss of bargaining power in supplier negotiation
Evaluation of designs/plans re supply factors and risks	Post-contract capability/relationship problems

Through the PURCHASING CYCLE:

1.	*Identify need*	Input to client re feasibility, sustainability, options
2.	*Develop business case*	Input to investment appraisal, constraints/assumptions
3.	*Define sourcing approach*	Input re supply market, relevant procurement policies, regulations and processes, make/do or buy decisions
4.	*Supplier appraisal*	Input re approved/potential suppliers, pre-qualification and tender requirements
5.	*Tender management*	Input re requirements for tender documentation, advertisement, evaluation of tenders, debriefs
6.	*Contract award*	Input re dialogue/clarification requirements, finalisation of contract documentation, authorisation
7.	*Contract management*	Input to contract management protocols and implementation
8.	*Closure and review*	Input to review, lesson documentation, feedback

Involving procurement staff... with appropriate expertise

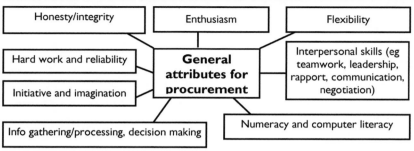

| Honesty/integrity | Enthusiasm | Flexibility |

| Hard work and reliability | **General attributes for procurement** | Interpersonal skills (eg teamwork, leadership, rapport, communication, negotiation) |
| Initiative and imagination | | |

| Info gathering/processing, decision making | Numeracy and computer literacy |

Procurement knowledge and expertise relevant to specific requirements: (**eg**)

❑ Supply market knowledge (relevant to procurement category)

❑ Product/category knowledge (relevant technologies, processes, market grades, national/international standards, regulations etc)

❑ Knowledge of customer/client objectives, requirements, constraints and decision-making processes and criteria

❑ Legal/commercial knowledge (regulations, incoterms, contract terms, dispute resolution mechanisms etc)

❑ Knowledge of all relevant procurement policies, guidelines and frameworks

❑ Expertise in procurement disciplines, processes and documentation (invitations to tender, specifications, compliant tender processes, negotiations, contracts and agreements, contract management etc)

❑ Expertise in use of e-sourcing and e-procurement tools

 Competencies are clusters of knowledge, skill and personal attributes that contribute to successful job performance. Competence frameworks often define adequate performance (at different levels) in terms of observable behaviours.

Key roles (units of competence)	**Eg MoD units of competence:**
Specific activities (elements of competence)	❑ Customer requirements
To what standard (outcomes)	❑ Market
At what level of development (eg awareness, practitioner, expert)	❑ Contractual negotiations
With what underpinning knowledge and 'core competencies' (general management skills)	❑ Contractual process
	❑ Procurement relationships

Evaluate the importance of involving procurement staff with expertise appropriate for the requirement at an early stage

1.4

Communication skills for procurement staff

 Communication is the transmission or exchange of information. It is best expressed as a *cyclical* or two-way process: eg the 'radio signal' model.

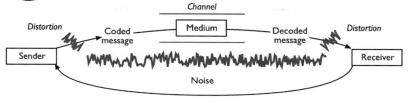

Feedback ('Message understood?')

Communication skills	Communication channels
First-order skills: rapport, active listening, empathy, using/interpreting non-verbal communication, using written formats, using communication tools	**Downwards**: manager to subordinate eg: Instructions, briefings, rules/policies, plans
	Lateral: cross functional eg: networking, project meetings, inter-department emails
Second-order skills: negotiation, influencing, conflict resolution, leadership, teamwork, consulting	**Upwards**: staff to management eg: reports, feedback, suggestions, upward appraisal

With more senior staff...	With different backgrounds...
Report by exception/variance and filter/summarise info: avoid info overload	Adapt to abilities, limitations, interests and objectives of target audience
Link info/proposals to relevant strategic objectives: present business case	Use active listening: ask supportive questions, check understanding, summarise
Use appropriate influencing techniques: rapport, rational persuasion, coalition	Supply supportive information (eg labelling of graphs, definitions, explanatory notes)
Be concise, relevant, professional, timely	Avoid 'jargon' (professional or technical)
Present balanced, structured arguments	

MAKING A BUSINESS CASE
- ❑ Summary of background to issue
- ❑ Business objectives attempting to achieve
- ❑ Outline of options to achieve objectives
- ❑ Identification of preferred option, with justification
- ❑ Plan of action, including milestones for progress measurement
- ❑ Summary of resources required + likely financial outcomes (cost/benefit)
- ❑ Measures of success used to monitor/control outcomes

Conventional (departmental budget) funding

The UK government's biennial **Spending Review** sets three-year departmental resource and capital budgets. **Departmental budgets** control spending of public sector organisations for which they are responsible.

☑ Usually lowest cost of capital (eg raised through taxation)
☑ Budgeting integrated with corporate planning
☑ Budgets include output and performance measures > control and accountability
☑ Forces prioritisation of projects

☒ Finite amount of capital available: major constraint on project initiation
☒ Up-front financial burden on taxpayer
☒ Public ownership of projects/assets may act as a constraint on innovation, change.

Private Finance Initiative (PFI)

The **Private Finance Initiative** (PFI) is a procurement structure which secures private funding for public institutions in return for part-privatisation.

• 30-60 year contract with a private sector consortium (Special Purpose Vehicle: SPV)
• May involve various combinations of finance, design, build, operate, maintain
• Scrutinised and reported on re VFM by UK National Audit Office

☑ Secures major capital funding (potentially enabling more large-scale projects)

☑ May access private sector expertise/technology in design, construction and operation
☑ Exploits and stimulates private sector innovation
☑ Enables faster completion > cost savings

☑ PFI projects do not appear as liability in public accounts (adding to government debt)

☒ Risk of surrendering control > lower public accountability (and levels of service?)
☒ If private sector operates service, may be TUPE issues of staff transfer
☒ Long-term contract: risk of 'lock in' with incompatible or underperforming partner
☒ Difficult to evaluate in terms of value for money

Bond financing

In finance, a **bond** is a debt security: the holder effectively 'lends' the issuer funds, on which the issuer is bound to pay interest (the coupon) and/or to repay the principal at a defined date (maturity). Bonds are issued by public authorities (as well as credit institutions and companies).

☑ Immediate method of raising finance
☑ Up-front financial burden on the taxpayer is reduced
☑ Repayment period can be very long-term

☒ Can create long-term costs
☒ Not efficient unless revenue stream supporting it is based on full marginal cost of project in which the investment is made.

Whole-life costing

Whole-life costing is 'the systematic consideration of all costs and revenues associated with the ownership of an asset... supporting decision-making in areas such as: investment appraisal and risk management; product/asset comparison; asset management planning; and 'make or buy' decisions.' *(CIPS)*

☑ Supports comparison of purchases with different life spans (eg as payback time)
☑ Supports business case for sustainable procurement (eg savings in running costs)
☑ Promotes communication between stakeholders in the purchase
☑ Supports risk management, realistic budgeting and value for money procurement

---

Determine **operating cycle** of equipment

$\downarrow$

Estimate **costs** (and benefits) of ownership arising **in each year** of useful life.
(Costs at current rates/prices > project to future dates at which incurred.)

$\downarrow$

Use **discounted cashflow** to calculate **net present value** of costs.
(Discount amounts to today's values.)   *See below*

$\downarrow$

Compute **annual equivalent cost** (cost of ownership of asset over one year)
> enables comparison of assets with different useful lives...

Investment appraisal   *(HM Treasury 'Green Book')*

Investment appraisal techniques are used to inform decisions about whether to invest in a capital project, or which capital projects to invest in.

Investment appraisal process (OGC Gateway):

❑ Identify need and business objectives
❑ Identify business options
❑ Assess quantitative costs and benefits of each option
❑ Assess qualititative benefits of each option (environmental, political, social benefits)
❑ Demonstrate effective risk mitigation strategy for each option
❑ Present results and recommend preferred option

Future cashflows associated with life of asset:

- *Cash outflows*: eg cost of capital equipment, loan interest payable, wages/salaries
- *Cash inflows*: eg increased revenue, savings in operating costs
- *Net cashflows*: cash inflows *minus* cash outflows for the period
- *Opportunity cost of capital*: benefit forgone by investing in this project, not another

>> Investment appraisal techniques to determine **net present value** of project.

Payback method

Assesses how long a project will take to 'pay back' the initial investment.

eg   Purchase of £200,000 machine > financial benefits of £50,000 pa over 5-year use.

	Net cashflow each year £	Cumulative cashflow £
Year 0	(200,000)	(200,000)
Year 1	50,000	(150,000) —— -ve cashflow only part offset
Year 2	50,000	(100,000)
Year 3	50,000	(50,000)
Year 4	50,000	0 —— Investment paid back
Year 5	50,000	50,000 —— Positive cashflow

☑ Simple to use, relatively 'safe': useful for screening potential projects
☒ Doesn't look at rate of return: only rapidity of re-payment

Accounting rate of return (ARR) method

Calculate average rate of return earned by money invested.

eg   Overall rate of return (£200,000 invested; £250,000 savings) = £50,000.
Average return (over 5 years) = £10,000 = 5% rate of return on £200,000 invested.

☑ Easy to compare for different projects to identify **best rate of return**
☒ Doesn't look at project life span or timing of cashflows

Discounted cashflow (DCF) techniques

Time value of money	• Preference for *receiving money now rather than in the future*. • Preference for *paying money in the future, rather than now*.
Present value	>> Calculate value in today's terms (**present value**) of money receivable/payable at future date: eg **discount** for interest lost/gained.
Net present value (NPV)	Discount estimated **net cashflows** for each year > **total present values** of all cashflows over life of project (NPV). • +ve NPV: project worth undertaking *or* • −ve NPV: project costs more than it is worth! • Project comparison: higher NPV is more attractive.
Internal rate of return (IRR)	IRR = % **discount rate at which NPV = 0** > ☑ or ☒ project. If firm can borrow at % *less* than IRR: IRR (return) = *greater* than cost of financing (**target/hurdle rate**) >> project viable.

☑ Takes account of lifecycle costs, actual cashflows, time value of money
☒ Subjective assumptions, uncertain future cashflows

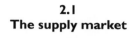

Evaluating the opportunities

2.1
The supply market

Course Book Chapter 6

- Changes to suppliers
- Technological changes
- Competition (Five Forces)

2.2
Aggregation and co-operative procurement

Course Book Chapter 7

- Aggregation of similar requirements
- EU and UK rules on aggregation
- Geographical scope of sourcing

2.3
Sustainable procurement

Course Book Chapter 8

- Environmental sustainability
- Ethical procurement
- Social sustainability of supply chain

2.0
Scope and nature of contract

Planning the contract

2.4
Contract duration and number of suppliers

Course Book Chapter 9

2.6
Intended costs and benefits from the contact

Course Book Chapter 10

- Source of info on costs/benefits
- Sharing costs/benefits
- Incentivisation

2.5
Involving stakeholders in contract specification

Course Book Chapter 9

- Types of specification
- Involving clients/potential suppliers
- Involving financial/technical experts

Evaluating the supply market

Purchasing research is a process of ongoing research into supply markets: to provide information for planning, so that the organisation can adapt to changes in the supply environment, and to support best value.

- Environmental analysis (PESTLE factors)
- Industry analysis (eg Porter's Five Forces)
- Vendor analysis: capacity and performance of potential and current suppliers
- Market analysis: structure of market; likely availability, prices etc

Aims of supply market evaluation	Sources of information
Support supply market strategies	Supply market sources
Identify opportunities, leverage points and threats arising from market factors	Trade directories and reports
	Supplier literature and website
Understand stakeholder perspectives	Previous contracts and agreements
Support negotiation and influencing	Supplier site visits and audits
Support risk management	The internet

Number and size of suppliers

Market structure refers to the number of organisations competing in a given supply market, giving rise to different forms of competition.

Decreasing competition →

Perfect competition	Monopolistic competition	Oligopoly	Monopoly
Many small sellers: no market power	Fewer small suppliers	Small number of large suppliers	One supplier only (single firm or cartel)
Homogeneous goods: perfect substitutes	Some difference: close substitutes	Differentiation, with variable substitution	One offering only: no close substitutes
Perfect market info	Imperfect info	Imperfect info	Imperfect info
No barriers/costs to entry or exit	No barriers to entry in long run	High barriers to entry	High barriers to entry
No switching barriers > 'market price': suppliers are 'price takers'	Differentiation may support price variations eg for brand/quality	Avoidance of price wars: > price collusion (and non-price competition)	Monopolist controls supply > power to determine market price ('price maker')
Buying implications: Ease of switching Wide supply base Known market price	*Buying implications:* Suppliers compete Seek 'best deal' Switching costs	*Buying implications:* Small supply base Collusion on price Seek non-price value	*Buying implications:* Potential high price Little or no choice Regulated market

Other issues in supplier size:
- ❑ Large contract > small-turnover supplier: risk of financial unsustainability
- ❑ Small contract > large-turnover supplier: risk of contract being low priority
- ❑ Number, skills, deployment of employees > measure of capacity/capability
- ❑ Sustainability: support for SMEs

Supplier location

- ❑ *Length of supply line*: impact on packaging/transport costs/risks, delivery lead times
- ❑ *International sourcing*: tariff and non-tariff costs of import; exchange rate risk; transport risk; difficulty monitoring ethical/quality standards; environmental impact of transport; different PESTLE factors – BUT potential value from resource/technology available, low-cost labour price savings, social sustainability in supporting developing economies
- ❑ *Local sourcing*: issues of skill/resource availability, possibly uncompetitive pricing – BUT social/economic sustainability (local employment/investment etc)
- ❑ *Service contracts*: proximity/accessibility to area of service provision > response times, costs, compatibility of language/culture etc.

Sustainability/socio-economic considerations

Sustainability policy > stimulate local/regional economies, supplier diversity > support for:

- ❑ *SMEs*: boosting employment and income distribution; encouraging entrepreneurship; supporting capacity building
- ❑ *Minority-owned businesses* (eg BMEs) and women-owned businesses: overcoming hurdles such as access to finance, capacity building
- ❑ *Social Enterprises* (SEs: businesses pursuing socially beneficial objectives). Supporting delivery of social policy objectives: capacity building, socially inclusive wealth creation, neighbourhood regeneration, innovation in public service provision, active citizenship.

Technological changes in the supply market

Change in production/supply processes (labour saving, healthy/safe, efficient, environmentally 'clean', flexible)

Influences supply market competition: eg increasing or lowering entry barriers

Potential for e-procurement platforms, improved supply market info/communication

Overview of technology factors

Raises issues: eg technology transfer, technology risk (viruses, breakdown etc), ethics (redundancies), cost

Opens up new supply markets: global access + economies

Raises productivity/capacity

Changes labour/skill requirements and organisation (eg 'virtual', outsourcing)

Shortens product lifecycles: pressure for continuous innovation

Q. Do technological changes/innovations offer:

❑ Cost-efficiencies + quality/service improvements > value for money?
❑ Innovative solutions to problems?
❑ Environmental/sustainability benefits (eg lower emissions, small supplier access)?
❑ More efficient ways of communicating with internal/external stakeholders (eg CRM)?

NB: implications/costs/risks for data security, staffing/organisation, decision-making...

Five Forces Model   *(Michael Porter)*

Porter's Five Forces Model: factors > intensity of competition in an industry.

- **Existing competitive rivalry.**
  Intense where: many equally balanced competitors; slow rate of industry growth; lack of differentiation; high fixed costs; high exit barriers.

- **Threat of new entrants.**
  '*Barriers to entry*': eg economies of scale, brand differentiation, high capital requirements, control over distribution channels, etc

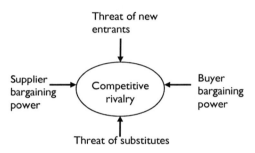

- **Threat from substitutes:** availability of alternative products that serve the same purpose > limits price that firm can charge for its products.

- **Bargaining power of buyers**: eg to force down prices. Relatively high when eg: buyers few; products undifferentiated (easy switching); spend is high proportion of suppliers' revenue; buyer owns/controls supplier.

- **Bargaining power of suppliers**: eg to raise prices. Relatively high when eg: suppliers few; few substitute products; product/service is important to buyers; supplier owns/controls buying firm.

STRATEGIES TO INCREASE THE POWER OF BUYERS:

❑ Consolidate/aggregate purchases > increase contract volume/value
❑ Consortium buying > increase contract volume/value
❑ Increase technical/negotiating skills in buying team
❑ Conduct purchasing research > promote wider informed choice, supply market competition
❑ Value analysis, variety reduction > support substitutes, ease of switching, competition
❑ Use smaller suppliers, for whom the contract is high priority
❑ Cultivate 'good customer' status: high value business + ethical/efficient dealings, prompt payment etc.

Consortium buying

 A **purchasing consortium** is a group of two or more independent organisations that join together to purchase goods or services > use combined buying power to obtain better terms in negotiation with suppliers.

Loose collective or local network	No formal structure: informal info sharing and aggregation of requirement for better pricing
Voluntary co-op or confederation	Formal or informal. Usually within a segment (eg health). Competitive sourcing based on aggregated definition of needs.
Regional purchasing agency	Central authority provides procurement services to public sector organisations (eg local authority purchasing consortium)
National purchasing agency	As regional, but managed on a national basis: may place handling charge on services (eg OGC Buying Solutions, NHS PASA)
Member-owned service orgs	Two or more institutions create a separate entity to provide services to participating organisations (usually segment specific)
Commercial consortia	For-profit entities: (a) purchasing goods based on aggregate demand of clients > resell at a profit OR (b) acting as a purchasing agent for clients and charging commission. Usually 'vertical' (within segment).

☑ Aggregated requirements > enhanced bargaining power + economies of scale
☑ Streamlined procurement processes > cost savings (esp for low-value items)
☑ Buyers freed up to prioritise more strategic categories
☑ Shared info on supply market, demand, best practice etc > purchasing improvements, best price/value, risk management
☑ Access to pooled specialist technical/commercial expertise

☒ Cost/effort of communication, co-ordination, staff development, policy development
☒ Potential member resistance re lack of control, 'lock in' to contract etc.
☒ Shared info > risk loss of confidentiality, control over intellectual property
☒ Supplier reluctance re reduced profit margins (despite larger volume)
☒ Difficulty allocating costs/burden and savings/discounts fairly among members
☒ Potential for lengthy procurement process > reduced efficiency, longer lead times
☒ May 'concentrate market power' > fall foul of UK/EU competition law
☒ May pose barriers to smaller suppliers > against sustainability/diversity policy
☒ May pose barriers to smaller, innovative suppliers > depressing innovation

EU and UK rules on aggregation

Aggregation rules and thresholds	Compulsory competitive tendering for all contracts above a defined financial threshold: • Aggregating estimated value of separate contracts for meeting a single requirement • Aggregating estimated value of series of contracts or renewable contract for supplies/services of same type in 12-month period

Framework agreements

 A **framework agreement** sets out terms and conditions under which specific purchases (call-offs) will be made from a given supplier during the term of the agreement.

☑ Cuts out time/admin involved in numerous small orders, negotiation of terms
☑ Usually removes requirement to advertise/tender each new requirement
☑ Mechanism for consortium buying by central purchasing bodies: individual members can call off supplies/services, as and when need arises
☑ Suits low-value, large-volume where exact timing/quantity is unknown (eg MRO)

☒ Needs to be handled properly (eg realistic estimates of annual requirements, realistic order lead times, consultation with all potential participants) > obtain agreement

EU Procurement Directive and UK Public Contracts Regulations 2006:

• Framework may last for up to four years.

• Names/type of organisations participating in framework agreement must be published in OJEU notice, other media and/or invitation to tender documentation.

• Participants may also have to complete an 'Access Agreement' to use framework.

Authority may enter into contracts by:

Applying agreed terms	[Requirement less than £50,000]: calling off orders from framework provider offering most economically advantageous offer in respect of particular requirement

Re-opening competition	[In relation to unfixed terms or requirements over £50,000]. • 'Mini-competition' between category suppliers within the framework, on basis of award criteria set out in agreement • Substantive modifications to framework terms not permitted: supplement or refine terms to reflect individual call-off needs (eg delivery time-scales, invoicing arrangements, associated services)

Nature of the client's requirements

Standard requirement	Added/amended features	Tailored for client
Straight call-off	Modified specification	New specification

- ❑ Standardisation of requirement is a key factor in successful aggregation > challenge of differing internal/external client requirements
- ❑ Centrally-managed contracts may not be responsive to needs of front-line staff (+ difficulty of gathering performance feedback)
- ❑ Difficult to specify standard requirement in a way that meets needs of all participants: whole-life value may be better achieved by contracting separately

Optimum geographic scope of sourcing/delivery

Benefits of local sourcing	Drawbacks of local sourcing
Investment in community, employment, skills (plus reputational/brand benefits)	Materials, skills or capabilities may not be available locally (or may be more costly)
Accessibility for supplier development and contract management (eg site visits)	Smaller suppliers: no economies of scale (higher costs), greater dependency issues
Supplier knowledge of local market, sustainability issues, regulatory standards	Local sourcing policy may make local suppliers complacent/un-competitive
Reduced transport, payment, cultural risks and costs	Public sector may not discriminate on basis of geography, over tendering thresholds
Short supply chain eg supporting JIT, fewer environmental impacts of transport	VFM issues: likely to be restricted to lower-value purchases

National/regional sourcing: larger requirements, or no suitable local supplier.
- ❑ Need to evaluate supplier capability; distribution network; accessibility; etc.
- ❑ Higher supply chain costs: minimise via accurate demand forecasting, transport planning etc.

Benefits of international sourcing	Drawbacks of international sourcing
Availability of required materials and/or skills: increased supply competitiveness	Exchange rate risk, currency management issues, high sourcing/transaction costs
Competitive price and cost savings (scale economies, low labour costs)	Cost savings and lower standards may create sustainability/reputational risk
Less onerous constraints/costs re environmental and labour compliance	Different legal frameworks, time zones, standards, language and culture
International trade promotes economic development, international relations etc	Additional risks: political, transport, payment, supplier standards monitoring
Public sector: compulsory to advertise contracts within the EU	Environmental impacts of transport/haulage (especially by air freight)

>> Need to develop strategies/policies taking both sides of argument into account – and carefully implemented/managed to minimise drawbacks/risks of chosen strategy.

Sustainable procurement

Sustainable procurement is 'a process whereby organisations meet their needs for goods, services, works and utilities in a way that achieves value for money on a whole-life basis in terms of generating benefits not only to the organisation, but also to society and the economy, whilst minimising damage to the environment' *(Sustainable Procurement National Action Plan)*

❑ *UK Sustainable Procurement Task Force* *(Procuring the Future, 2006)*: public sector leadership by example; integrated policy framework; raising of minimum standards; building capacity; removing barriers; capturing opportunities for innovation; a Flexible Framework for implementation and improvement.

Sustainability =	Economic	Environmental	Social

ISSUES IN PUBLIC SECTOR SUSTAINABLE PROCUREMENT:

☑ Commitment to public sector leadership in sustainable procurement/consumption

☑ Local, national and international sustainability treaties (eg Kyoto), legislation, policies (eg National Action Plan) and agendas (eg Local Agenda 21)

☑ Opportunities for sustainable procurement: challenge sustainability of client requirements; sustainable purchase specifications; sustainable sourcing (including social and environmental sustainability criteria for pre-qualifying suppliers); whole-life costing, contract and impacts management; developing suppliers for sustainability; monitoring and improving sustainable procurement performance

☒ Perceived conflict between Value for Money policy, efficiency agenda, budgetary constraints **vs** higher costs of sustainable products/services. Need for re-definition of 'value'; whole-life costing to highlight potential for sustainability efficiencies and cost savings; rationalisation of policies and priorities

☒ EU Public Procurement framework restricts contract award criteria (most economically advantageous tender, direct relevance to subject matter of contract). Need for social and environmental sustainability criteria to be built into early stages of business case, specification, supplier pre-qualification.

Sustainable Procurement National Action Plan:

1. Benchmark performance: identify improvement areas (eg using Flexible Framework: tool to locate organisations against five levels of performance in five key areas)

2. Identify priority areas of spend (based on risk assessment)

3. Rethink requirements: analyse business need

4. Engage stakeholders in design specification (eg early supplier/contractor involvement)

5. Aggregate demand (across organisation, through buyers, over time)

6. Use Quick Wins and Common Minimum Standards (guidelines for immediate gains)

7. Ensure management info systems are in place to measure sustainability benefits

Green procurement

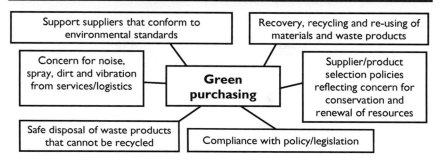

Support suppliers that conform to environmental standards

Recovery, recycling and re-using of materials and waste products

Concern for noise, spray, dirt and vibration from services/logistics

Green purchasing

Supplier/product selection policies reflecting concern for conservation and renewal of resources

Safe disposal of waste products that cannot be recycled

Compliance with policy/legislation

Some key environ-mental issues	• Scarce, non-renewable resources: reduce consumption rate and/or support renewable alternatives; ensure renewable resources (eg forests, fish stocks) managed sustainably • Climate change: reduce greenhouse gas emissions (eg by reduced energy/transport use; purchase of green products)
Energy efficiency	Fossil fuel depletion > rising energy costs. Need for: • Reduced energy consumption via usage patterns (eg transport) • Specification of energy efficient plant/equipment/services • Investment in alternative/renewable energy sources
Recycling	Reducing waste to landfill eg by reduction, re-use, recycling policies. • Supplier reverse logistics: take-back for recycling • Design/specification for disassembly, recyclability • Promoting recycling practices with clients, staff, public
Biodegrad-ability	Reducing non-bio-degradable waste (eg plastics) to landfill. • Specification of biodegradable materials where possible

Ethical procurement

CSR promotes the integration of stakeholder issues into business operations... treating stakeholders ethically or in a responsible manner... to produce an overall positive impact on society. *(CIPS)*

Purchasing contribution to ethical/CSR objectives:

❑ Adhere to relevant Codes of Practice and CIPS ethical code (eg re disclosure of interests, confidentiality, inducements/corruption)
❑ Adhere to global standards (eg Ethical Trading Initiative) re human/labour rights
❑ Enforce/support ethical practices and standards by suppliers
❑ Adhere to health and safety, equal opportunity and ethical employment practices
❑ Adopt Fair Trade principles (consistent with VFM and supplier selection rules)
❑ Support fair competition (in compliance with EU Procurement Directives)

❑ **Fair trade:** policies aimed at ethical treatment and payment of producers and workers in developing countries; supporting disadvantaged producers in accessing international markets. Public sector organisations may obtain accredited Fair Trade products, where consistent with VFM policy and award criteria rules

Enhancing supplier access

Social legislation (eg on equality and diversity) and sustainable procurement policy supports enhanced access to public sector contracts by SMEs, SEs, BMEs, women- and disabled-owned businesses, and Voluntary and Community Services (VCS) suppliers.

☑ Represent diversity of society: encouraging wider access to services, social inclusion
☑ Increased competition > value for money benefits to contracting authorities
☑ May offer innovative, responsive solutions (with support for capacity building)
☑ May be well placed to deliver services to hard-to-reach areas, segments

---

EU/UK rules on social/environmental criteria in contract award:

- Criteria must be 'linked to the subject-matter of the contract' (EU directive Recital 1)

- 'A contracting authority may use criteria aiming to meet social requirements, in response in particular to the needs – defined in the specifications of the contract – of particularly disadvantaged groups of people to which those receiving/using the works, suppliers or services which are the object of the contract belong' (Recital 46)

- Scope to include social policy criteria during requirement definition, specification, contract development, contract management

- Scope to support small/minority suppliers with briefing, training, information-sharing and capacity building

---

Mechanisms for enhancing access:

Splitting large contracts	Geographically or by category, to suit small supplier capacity and/or specialist capability (and bring below open tender threshold, where relevant)
Preference schemes	EU Directive Article 19: option to reserve contracts for organisations providing supported employment opportunities to disabled people ('supported factories and businesses') > open competition between pre-qualified organisations.
Outreach schemes	Access to info/support for small/diverse suppliers eg: • Meet the Buyer events: networking, discussion of potential opportunities, criteria, procurement procedures etc • Internet: eg details of low-value contracts advertised on supply2gov.uk, small business info services, procurement agency websites • Business Link information and support services • Multi-lingual procurement info, tender/contract documentation

Planning contract duration

Total anticipated duration: including contracting period + options to renew.

- ❑ Matching anticipated need for commodities/services
- ❑ Consistent with best value procurement principles
- ❑ Clearly and explicitly stated in the contract
- ❑ Incorporating performance/improvement measures, review/renegotiation options

Factors impacting on contract duration

Duration of requirement	Long-term services required by statute/policy + nature not changeable (eg audit services): better value from long-term contract
	Medium-term services with high initial supplier input (eg training): medium-term contract (2–3 years) for flexibility
Market features	Immature/volatile markets: short/medium contracts to allow for risk, change, innovation, early high costs
	Mature/stable markets: value from long-term contracts with well established suppliers
Technology change	Fast-changing technological environment: provision for contract to be reviewed/modified/terminated in event of change leading to obsolescence or unforeseen costs
Price stability	Price stability: long-term contract advantageous to buyer + supplier (but allow for market test or benchmark to ensure ongoing VFM)
	Price volatility: short-term contracts to exploit low/falling prices
Capacity	Need to ensure supplier capacity/resources to fulfil long contract
	Market capacity > competitive pricing: short contracts to exploit
Storage	Efficiency: hold as little stock as possible. Long-term contracts: supplier holds consignment stock (for call-off)
EU/UK rules & policy	'Balance between competitive value of short-term contracts and stability, continuity and potentially lower yearly costs of a long-term contract' (OGC guidance)
	EU directive: framework agreements not to exceed 4 years
Supplier relationships	Close, positive, collaborative supplier relations and contract management required for success of long contracts
	Transactional relationships: less trust, mutual adaptation etc > more suited to short contracts

Drivers for longer-term contracts:

- ❑ Capital and switching costs
- ❑ Continuity of service issues (stability needs, knowledge transfer etc)
- ❑ Market volatility and risk: need to secure supply
- ❑ Benefits of continuous improvement, relationship/supplier development over time

Constraints on long-term contracts:
- ❑ Commitment to longer-term funding and programme decisions; funding stability
- ❑ Change in nature of commodities/services being procured
- ❑ Capability of staff to plan/negotiate long-term agreements up front
- ❑ Availability of flexible contract management systems to support long-term contracts

Factors influencing the optimum number of suppliers

Wide supply base: competition supports VFM, reduces risk of dependency	**Narrow supply base:** lower transaction costs, potential for relationship development

Capacity of the market	Number of suppliers required/able to produce volume of requirement
Impact on competition	Narrow supply base may depress competition: obligation to open contracts to wider supply market Wide supply base intensifies competition > price/value opportunity
Range of products/ services included	More complex range of products/services: fewer suppliers able to meet full spectrum of need. Aggregate requirement: larger orders to fewer suppliers > economy of scale, procurement efficiencies Dis-aggregate requirement: smaller orders to more suppliers (eg for improved specialisation, access for small/minority suppliers)
Ease of supply chain management	Smaller supply base: easier contract and supply chain management (especially complex, international supply chains) > reduced cost and risk (eg of supply/project failure, reputational damage etc)
Number/ location of customers & delivery points	Wide supply base may be required to reach geographically dispersed customers, hard-to-reach areas: need for proximity of customers to delivery points. Will depend on suppliers' demonstrated logistics capability/structure, distribution network etc.
Scope for SME/minority access	Wider supply base of smaller/diverse suppliers (where required, by dis-aggregation of requirement) may be required to support policy of access to SME/minority businesses
Risk of too few suppliers	Too few available/pre-qualified suppliers: risk of buyer over-dependency. Vulnerability to supplier failure or supply disruption; complacent, un-competitive performance or pricing; etc

A **specification** is a statement of the requirements to be satisfied in the supply of a product or service.

☑ **Defines the requirement:** making stakeholders consider what they really need

☑ **Communicates the requirement** clearly to suppliers, so they can plan to conform (and/or come up with more innovative or lower-cost solutions)

☑ **Defines quality** (conformance to spec) for evaluation of goods/services supplied.

Types of specifications

Conformance/technical spec	Performance (functional) spec
Buyer details what product, part or material must *consist of*.	Buyer details what product, part or material must *be able to do or achieve*.
Eg: blueprint, chemical formula, sample for duplication.	Eg: statement of functions to be performed, levels of performance to be reached.
Supplier's task is to *conform* to prescription/description given by buyer.	Supplier's task is to provide solutions that *fulfil specified ends* - with flexibility re means.
☑ Precise, detailed info re requirement ☑ Fair competition between suppliers ☑ Precise standard for evaluation ☑ Minimise risk where buyer has more technical expertise than suppliers ☒ Time-consuming and costly to draft ☒ Buyer bears risk of design not performing ☒ May restrict choice of supplier, access by small suppliers ☒ Prescriptive nature may restrict innovation, lower-cost options etc	☑ Easier/cheaper than conformance ☑ Exploits expertise, technology and innovative capacity of suppliers ☑ Wider supply base: range of solutions ☑ Supplier responsibility for functionality Particularly appropriate where: ☑ Suppliers have technical expertise ☑ Rapid technology change: buyer gets 'up to date' solutions ☑ Clear criteria to evaluate options ☑ Buyer has time/expertise to evaluate proposals

Involving clients at an early stage of specification

☑ Definition of value according to user needs
☑ Improved acceptance by clients/users
☑ Improved likelihood of effective implementation by clients/users
☑ Opportunity to challenge client definition of requirement + gain acceptance

Involving potential suppliers at an early stage of specification

Early supplier involvement (ESI) is a process whereby suppliers are involved at an early stage in the product/service development process, making proactive suggestions to improve designs and materials specifications.

- ☑ Providing constructive criticism of designs; suggesting alternative materials or manufacturing methods – at a time when changes are still possible.
- ☑ Quicker development lead time
- ☑ Shared expertise for problem-solving, innovation
- ☑ Mutual understanding of requirements

Under EU Public Procurement Directives (UK Public Contracts Regulations), **competitive dialogue** is permitted for complex contracts: process conducted in successive stages to identify potential solutions and gradually reduce number of tenders.

Accessing expertise for developing and managing specification

Technical experts (eg in IT, construction, health) contribute:

- ☑ Advice on manufacturing processes, quality management processes, world class standards, innovation
- ☑ Ability to define technical specs
- ☑ Ability to evaluate technical content of pre-qualification responses
- ☑ Support for resolution of technical disputes, continuous improvement
- ☒ Temptation to over-specify
- ☒ Narrow specs reduce supply options

Financial experts (eg in financing, financial planning/management, accounting and reporting) contribute to:

- Project budgeting, analysis, investment appraisal, whole-life costings etc
- Costs and methods of financing
- Structure of PFI contracts
- Estimate of liquidated damages etc
- Development of cost models and price review mechanisms
- Financial appraisal of accounts
- ☒ May under-prioritise non-monetary factors in 'value' (eg sustainability)

Procurement contributes:

- ☑ Supply market awareness (potential suppliers, generic options, risk factors etc)
- ☑ Purchasing disciplines > variety/cost reduction, value analysis etc
- ☑ Evaluation of designs re supply factors

Other government bodies (eg OCG, HM Treasury, Environment Agency)

Suppliers and supply market contacts

External advisory bodies (professional bodies, NGOs)

Sources of expertise

In-house consultants, functional specialists or cross-functional team

External consultancies
Need for: clear business case; 'terms of reference' brief; evaluation of selection factors; contract/performance monitoring and review

Cross functional teamworking

Multi-disciplinary or cross-functional teams (eg project teams) are teams which bring together individuals with different skills/specialisms, so that there competencies and resources can be pooled or exchanged, and/or so that their (potentially divergent) goals and interests can be represented.

Reasons for increased cross-functional teamworking:

❑ Increasing involvement of procurement staff in strategic procurement decisions
❑ Increasing adoption of supply chain philosophy > need for integrated work flow
❑ Makes best use of developments in ICT
❑ World class systems (eg MRP, TQM) require teamwork for implementation
❑ Global market/technology development etc > need for diverse expert input
❑ Multiple stakeholders > need for representation.

Advantages of cross-functional teamworking

☑ Better awareness of 'big picture'
☑ Reduction in time to get things done (via co-ordinated effort)
☑ Improved ability to solve complex problems, with multi-disciplinary input
☑ Improvement in organisation's customer/client/stakeholder focus (less emphasis on functional interests/priorities
☑ Improved creativity, innovation, learning (via multi-disciplinary interaction)
☑ Representation of stakeholder views/interests

Managerial challenges of cross-functional teamworking

☒ Complexity/conflict of interactions, different interests/priorities
☒ Ambiguous authority structures (where not a permanent structure)
☒ Lack of time to develop trust, seek consensus (eg in temporary task forces)
☒ Practical difficulties of meeting, info sharing etc (especially in multi-site organisations)

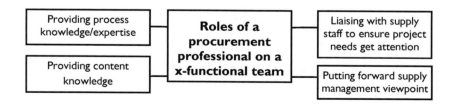

| Providing process knowledge/expertise | **Roles of a procurement professional on a x-functional team** | Liaising with supply staff to ensure project needs get attention |
| Providing content knowledge | | Putting forward supply management viewpoint |

Cost/benefit analysis

>> **Deciding on feasibility/value of requirement**

TOTAL COSTS	(direct, proportion of indirect, opportunity cost
÷	etc over lifetime of asset: total costs of acquisition, incl. maintenance, staffing, operation, disposal etc)
TOTAL BENEFITS PER YEAR	(of useful life, quantitative and qualitative, estimated
=	as a monetary value: eg revenue/profit potential, efficiencies, cost savings, client satisfaction, organisational learning, sustainability gains)
PAYBACK TIME	(period within which benefits will repay costs)

>> Go ahead if payback period acceptably short.

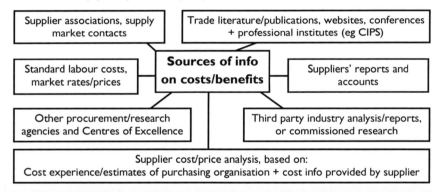

Sharing benefits and costs from the contract

Constructive ongoing supply relationships depend on equitable sharing of benefits/gains and risks/costs of contract – balanced with organisation's need to appropriate value, according to:

Nature of purchase (eg using Kraljic matrix)	• **Routine items** (low value, low supply risk): arms' length purchasing (eg blanket ordering) to secure lowest cost • **Leverage items** (high value, low risk): use adversarial approach, market dominance to secure best share of value • **Bottleneck items** (low value, high risk: delays if unavailable): share costs/benefits with suppliers as incentive/support for service and supply continuity • **Strategic items** (high value, high risk): focus on long-term total cost, security and competitiveness of supply >> long-term partnership relationships based on equitable cost/benefit sharing

Nature of relationship	Long-term partnership relationships based on mutual benefit, trust, development > cost/risk/gain sharing, incentivised contracts
	Short-term transactional relationships: maximise own share of value, within fair trade, CSR and sustainability policy framework

Cost of provision	Lower-value requirements unlikely to justify investment in incentives, gain/risk sharing agreements

Nature/ allocation of risks	Incentives/gain allocation should be fairly proportional to risk bearing. In partnership, risk register shared between client/contractor > joint approach to risk identification/sharing/mitigation.

Opportunities for incentivisation of suppliers

An **incentive contract** might be used where there is uncertainty about costs (too great for the supplier to agree to a fixed-price contract, but too little to justify a cost price adjustment clause) *and* the supplier can influence costs through efficiency, expertise and commitment.

❑ Agreement on: target cost for contract; target fee paid to supplier if target cost met; share formula (proportion of risk of cost variation borne by each party)

❑ Supplier incentive to keep actual costs below target cost: target cost + target fee + proportion of cost under-run (as determined by share formula)

Gainsharing is an approach to encourage cost reduction by suppliers, whereby the contract allows the supplier to retain a defined proportion of any cost reduction initiative that positively impacts the client/customer.

Advantages of gainsharing	Disadvantages of gainsharing
Win-win approach to negotiation	Requires ongoing management resource
Collaborative improvement-seeking	Requires transparent, quantifiable results
Focus on supply chain productivity	Requires high mutual trust
Flexibility: negotiated to suit contract	Frustration: circumstances beyond control
Can improve both party performance	Not justified by low-level purchases

Other approaches to supplier incentivisation:

❑ Guaranteed or fixed levels of capacity (allowing planning of investment/improvement)

❑ Opportunity for innovation: chance to develop marketable solutions

❑ Key performance indicators (KPIs) and targets for recognition (eg approved supplier status, supplier awards, bonuses or incentive payments)

❑ Continuous improvement agreements and/or capped price decreasing year on year

❑ Penalty clauses: unenforceable in practice

Allocation of responsibility for monitoring and reporting

 Contract management enables and ensures that both parties to a contract meet their obligations and deliver the outputs required from the contract.

Allocation of responsibility for progress/performance monitoring and reporting (v contract terms, service level agreements, KPIs etc) based on eg:

❑ Established contract management structure: contract/account management, cross-organisational contract management team, single/multiple points of contact etc.

❑ Predictability/volatility of performance/conditions

❑ Level of trust between client and contractor

❑ Balance of risk/responsibility for performance

❑ Accessibility, skills, resources and systems available for monitoring/reporting

❑ Need for third-party involvement (eg for standards accreditation, verification, overseas suppliers)

Management and operational information required

Performance v target (KPIs)	Managerial control: comparison of results v target > adjustment
	Basic performance measurement/management: reports against KPIs for cost, quality, delivery performance
Performance v critical targets or 'gates'	Project management: performance tested v critical targets/'gates', assessing ability to progress successfully to next stage > 'pass' or require correction
Progress v milestones	Project management: progress tested at pre-defined points ('milestones') for schedule/cost variance
Timeliness of reporting	Performance reports at contractually agreed times/intervals, eg:
	• Monthly performance reports (milestone achievement, status reports, progress v KPIs for the month)
	• Quarterly or end-stage reports (KPI trend analysis)
	• Annual service review (VFM reports; continuous improvement reports; feedback on customer satisfaction targets; benchmarking reports; efficiency/effectiveness targets)
Problem-solving and dispute resolution	Identification of potential issues: misunderstandings over terms, emerging problems/risks, missed deadlines, critical incident reporting etc.
	Defined governance arrangements and escalation processes for referring unresolved problems and disputes to higher levels
	Defined formal dispute resolution process (where possible based on Alternative Dispute Resolution: conciliation, arbitration)

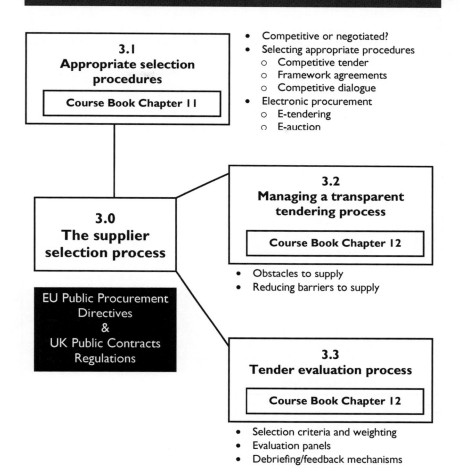

3.1
Appropriate selection procedures

Course Book Chapter 11

- Competitive or negotiated?
- Selecting appropriate procedures
  o Competitive tender
  o Framework agreements
  o Competitive dialogue
- Electronic procurement
  o E-tendering
  o E-auction

3.0
The supplier selection process

EU Public Procurement Directives
&
UK Public Contracts Regulations

3.2
Managing a transparent tendering process

Course Book Chapter 12

- Obstacles to supply
- Reducing barriers to supply

3.3
Tender evaluation process

Course Book Chapter 12

- Selection criteria and weighting
- Evaluation panels
- Debriefing/feedback mechanisms

Rules and policy on supplier selection procedures

Public Sector Directive (2004/18EC) > UK Public Contracts Regulations 2006:

➢ Open up choice of potential suppliers to public sector and utilities > reduced cost
➢ Ensure public sector purchasing decisions based on value for money via competition
➢ Ensure public sector bodies award contracts efficiently and without discrimination

Apply to purchasing by public bodies *unless* below defined **financial thresholds**.

Advertising	Subject to exceptions, public bodies must use **open tendering**: invitation to tender advertised for maximum publicity across member states, including publication of Contract Notice in the OJEU.

Selection procedures	• **Open procedure:** no requirement for pre-qualification of suppliers. Contract advertisement in OJEU: all respondents permitted to tender.
	• **Restricted procedure:** pre-qualification of suppliers permitted (technical and economic competence) + indication of predetermined range of suppliers (5–20) to whom tenders will be sent.
	• **Negotiated procedure:** Without call for competition: direct negotiation with chosen/existing supplier. With call for competition: pre-qualification + invitation to negotiate: not less than 3 parties selected to negotiate. May only be used in specific exceptional cases: emergency, exclusive rights, additional contracts, technical reasons, no appropriate tenders under other procedures.
	• **Competitive dialogue** (for complex contracts, where contract cannot be awarded under open/restricted procedure). Advertisement of requirement > technical dialogue for preparing specification > selection of firms invited to competitive dialogue (min 3) > competitive dialogue to develop solutions > submission of final tenders.

Framework agreements	Agreements with suppliers to establish the terms governing contracts to be awarded during a period (up to four years).

Electronic selection systems	• **Dynamic purchasing system:** completely electronic system, set up for a limited duration (up to 4 years), for making commonly-used purchases. Open throughout its duration to any pre-qualified supplier whose 'indicative tender' satisfies the criteria.
	• **Electronic auctions:** after full tender evaluation, electronic ranking of revised price/quality elements.

Utilities Directive > Public Utilities Regulations 2006

- Financial thresholds
- *No* competitive dialogue: utilities have greater scope to use negotiated procedures
- Exemption mechanism: where utility activity subject to competition, need not comply

Appropriateness of various selection procedures

Single tendering	Must be justified on VFM and agreed at appropriate level. • Low-value, low-risk purchases (eg using procurement card) • Higher-value purchases where only one supplier available • 'Additional' contract: supplier tendered for similar requirement within past 6 months • Emergency requirement (eg natural disaster) • Requirement for intellectual property owned by supplier ☑ Reduces procurement time, cost ☒ Difficult to justify non-competition: above thresholds, must fall within specified exemptions.
Open tendering	☑ Most effective where supply market small but competitive ☒ Cost, time, admin burden for authority and supply market ☒ No pre-qualification of potential bidders > risk
Restricted tendering	Most commonly used process (below and above thresholds) ☑ Allows pre-qualification: reduced time/cost, better quality bids ☑ Suitable where supply market large and competitive (wide range of goods and services)
Negotiated procedures	☑ Tried/tested: has market confidence, case law clarification ☑ Suitable where negotiation required to arrive at best value ☑ Cost-effective for both parties > VFM ☒ Difficult to justify under EU rules: subject to challenge ☒ Unstructured: risk of failure to comply with instructions ☒ De-selection generally at late stage > cost implications
Competitive dialogue	☑ Easily justified under EU rules ☑ Flexibility for complex contracts (where authority not able to define requirements of contract in terms of technical standards) ☑ Tests feasibility prior to commitment ☑ Collaborative solutions > innovation ☑ Saves cost of wider/irrelevant tender ☑ Specs, cost models etc developed ☒ New: little 'best practice' to go on ☒ Bidder reluctance to divulge confidential ideas, solutions ☑ High investment in process for unsuccessful bidders

Electronic procurement

E-tendering is the carrying out of competitive tendering process using electronic means (eg the internet and specialist software): advertisement of requirement, contract notice, document production, supplier registration, bid 'opening'/evaluation, notification of deadlines, notification of contract award.

Public Contracts Regulations 2006:

- **Devices** used must be able to guarantee: legal electronic signature; time/date stamping of actions; and strict control of access to transmitted and submitted data.

- **Time limits** may be shortened where contract notices are transmitted electronically or authority offers direct online access to documents.

☑ Facilitates management and co-ordination of tendering process > process efficiencies, freeing of procurement staff for more strategic value-adding activity
☑ Facilitates cross-functional communication
☑ Increases fairness and transparency of tendering process to suppliers
☑ Supports contract auditing, tender reporting/review/improvement

☒ Technical nature and costs of process may disadvantage some suppliers
☒ Perceived risks to data security/integrity

E-auctions are online reverse auctions, whereby suppliers use electronic systems to bid competitively on a contract over a specified bidding period.

Public Contracts Regulations 2006:

- 'Use of an electronic device for presentation of new *prices,* revised downwards, and/or new *values* concerning [non-price] elements of tenders, which occurs *after* an initial full evaluation of tenders, enabling them to be ranked using automatic evaluation methods.'

- All communication with bidders must be instantaneous (electronic)

- Only price/quality elements which can be used in a formula can be included at auction stage: other aspects must be addressed prior to auction.

☑ Save final negotiation time for buyers > focus on more strategic activities
☑ Cost savings from automation of processes (supplier and buyer)
☑ Suitable for easily specified, easily sourced goods: focus on best price
☑ Below EU thresholds: best-price, efficient approach to arm's length purchasing; ensures existing suppliers still competitive; makes true market price and price differentials transparent

☒ Set-up and integration costs offset potential savings
☒ Technique over-used at expense of supplier relationships and non-price criteria
☒ Not suitable for complex projects requiring dialogue, collaboration, negotiation
☒ Need to pre-qualify suppliers (if auction does not follow full tender evaluation)

Obstacles to accessing public procurement

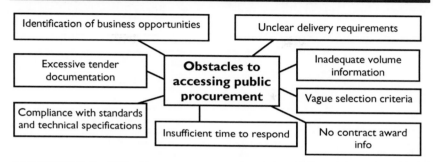

Identification of business opportunities	Cost of monitoring opportunities via publications; use of subscription/tracking services No central source for info re contract opportunities
Excessive tender docs	Cost and admin burden of pre-qualification, multiple questionnaires etc – with no guarantee of opportunity to quote/tender.
Compliance burden	Use of national/international standards and prescriptive technical specs puts compliance beyond the reach of smaller suppliers
Unclear delivery requirement	Where requirements are aggregated, there may be lack of clarity re delivery points: difficult to plan logistics. Framework agreements: uncertainty re timing of requirements.
Inadequate volume info	Devolved structures, framework agreements > broad estimate of likely volume requirements: difficult for suppliers to cost accurately
Vague selection criteria	Public Contracts Regs 2006: evaluation criteria and weightings published early *[>> Unit 3.3]*. But for low-value contracts, lack of clarity re price/non-price criteria > frustration in preparing bids, suspicion that process favours particular suppliers, frustration at lack of ability to communicate/clarify during tender process.
Insufficient response time	Public Contracts Regs 2006: minimum response times. But may still be unrealistic, given complexity of tender documentation > burden on bidders, frustration at missed deadlines, disincentive to bid.
No contract award info	Public Contracts Regs 2006: requirement to publish contract award notices, de-brief unsuccessful bidders. Below threshold, frustration at lack of notification, feedback, learning for future bids.

Reducing barriers to supply

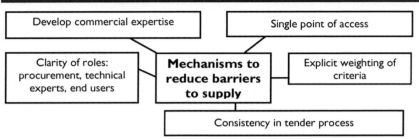

Develop commercial expertise	Develop commercial expertise of procurement staff for administering tenders, evaluations, de-briefs etc. Facilitate understanding with supply market: eg 'Meet the buyer', supplier open days, selling guides, procurement policy briefings etc.
Clarity of roles	Improve quality of tender information and streamline process by clarifying cross-functional roles in specification of requirement, evaluation of tender: remove ambiguities, conflicting requirements, uncertain points of contact/query etc.
Consistency of tender process	Improve perceived accessibility/fairness and supplier ability to learn and improve. Consistency in procedures/terminology/criteria used; supplier info on how to access process; streamlining of process (eg once-only pre-qualification); consistent access to debriefs; circulation of questions/clarifications arising in course of the bid.
Single point of access	Avoiding inefficiency of multiple/unclear points of contact/access. Eg via central purchasing body or e-procurement platform; single point of contact (procurement function) for submissions, queries etc
Explicit weighting of criteria [>> *Unit 3.3]*	Explicit publication of selection criteria + how they are defined + what value (weighting) they will be given in contract award. Especially important for non-price criteria (eg quality, sustainability) to justify 'best value'. ☑ Helps suppliers in formulation of effective bid ☑ Helps authority define requirement accurately ☑ Less waste of time/resource evaluating bids irrelevant to requirement.

Rules on selection criteria and weighting

Specification stage	• Avoid brand names and other references which would favour or disadvantage particular providers, products or services • Specify and accept 'equivalence' • Performance specifications may be used • Environmental/Fair Trade issues addressed in defined ways
Pre-qualification/ selection stage	*Exclusion* of prospective tenderers on defined criteria re: • **Suitability** (eg if found to have committed professional misconduct) • **Capacity** to perform the contract, based on evidence in regard to: economic/financial standing *and/or* technical/ professional capacity/competence.
Contract award stage	• Contracts should be let on basis of **objective** award criteria ensuring transparency, non-discrimination, equal treatment and competition. • Buyers generally obliged to award contract on basis of lowest price *or* [UK government policy] defined criteria for '**most economically advantageous tender**' (value for money). • All tenderers must have reasonable, *equal, timely information* re **criteria and weighting** of price and non-price criteria • Criteria/weightings must be **related to** 'purpose, nature, quantity or importance of the contract' • Criteria/weightings must **not discriminate** for/against particular suppliers (eg by restricting types of evidence of technical ability) or tenderers from other EU member states.

Selection criteria for various requirements

Category	Examples of criteria
Personal position	Exclude from selection on grounds of: bankruptcy, default on taxes, serious misrepresentation, grave misconduct
Economic and financial standing	Financial status Insurance provisions
Technical capacity and ability	Resources/technology/capacity Past performance; references from other clients Partnering Risk, quality, supply chain, environmental management systems Ethical/CSR/diversity/sustainability policies Rejected claims history (construction and engineering projects)

Use of weightings:

Selection criteria	Quality threshold	Weighting % (A)	Score awarded (B)	Weighted score (AxB)
Technical suitability	15	20	80	16
Risk management	4	10	50	5
Approach to partnering	6	15	60	9
Project-relevant resources	5	25	40	10
Specialist design experience	15	22	75	16.5
Quality assurance	5	8	80	6.4
Total weighting	50	100	Total	62.9

Award criteria must be:

❑ Specifically selected for **relevance/importance to the specific requirement**

❑ In line with **policies re socio-economic and environmental sustainability** eg:

- Accessibility to SMEs and minority businesses
- Addressing whole-life issues/costs of contract
- Stipulating environmental performance criteria
- Indicating that Fair Trade options will be welcome   *[>> Unit 2.3]*

Tender evaluation

ROLES/PROCEDURES OF EVALUATION PANEL

- Reviewing draft versions of tender documentation
- Commenting upon evaluation criteria and weightings
- Preparing realistic timetable for tender
- Evaluating written tenders v agreed criteria > shortlist best suppliers
- Attending shortlisted supplier presentations and participating in post-tender negotiation (where permitted for bid clarification purposes)
- Agreeing recommendation for contract award
- Maintaining records of the bid process

❑ **Constitution issues:** need to represent areas of expertise required for tender evaluation; need for stable membership over bid process

❑ **Ethical issues:** confidentiality of info; no prior release of info transmitted; no prior access to info submitted; exclusion from panel where conflicts of interest (eg relationship with supplier); no acceptance of inducements to influence contract award; objectivity of selection decisions

❑ **Procedures:** as defined by contracting body. Eg use of two-envelope tendering (quality and price elements of tender submitted and evaluated separately: shortlist suppliers on quality, compete on price); rejection of abnormally low tenders etc.

Mechanisms for contract award and providing feedback

Public Contracts Regulations 2006:

- Results/contract award notified to the Office of Official Publications of EC.

- Unsuccessful bidders have right to **debrief** within 48 days of request.

  ☑ Establish reputation as fair, honest, open and ethical client
  ☑ Benefit > unsuccessful bidder from time/money spent on process
  ☑ Builds capacity by enabling unsuccessful bidders to learn, improve
  ☑ Improves access to public sector contracts for small/minority suppliers

  > **General agenda for debriefing:**
  > ❑ Welcome and introduction
  > ❑ Description of evaluation process
  > ❑ Debrief: highlighting strengths and weaknesses of tender
  > ❑ Discussion of points
  > ❑ Closing statement from supplier
  > ❑ Feedback on the procurement process
  > ❑ Closing statement from the project team
  >
  > **Topics covered in debriefing** (UK Office of Govt. Commerce):
  >
  > | | |
  > |---|---|
  > | Cost ranking | Length of schedules |
  > | Design deficiencies | Organisation/administration |
  > | Experience | Personnel/management |
  > | Facilities and equipment | Subcontracting |
  > | Industrial relations record | Controls (cost/quality/schedule) |
  > | Contract terms | After-sales service |
  >
  > **Recommendations for debriefing** (UK Inland Revenue):
  > ❑ Don't disclose info re other tenderers > breach commercial confidentiality
  > ❑ Don't argue/justify award of contract to particular tenderer
  > ❑ Focus on weaknesses that led to rejection of unsuccessful bid
  > ❑ Give positive feedback on strengths of unsuccessful tenderer
  > ❑ Ask for supplier's feedback on debriefing process > improve

- **Alcatel period**: 10 day 'stand still' period between contract award and execution, in order to allow for legal challenge by unsuccessful bidders, in case of procedural irregularity (suspending contract).

NB De-briefing of *successful* tenderers also useful:

☑ Identify areas of tender strength > ensure they are delivered during term of contract

☑ Identify areas of tender weakness > ensure that they are addressed during term of contract, in continuous improvement planning (and/or in future tenders)

☑ Gather feedback on procurement process, how perceived from supplier side > process reporting, learning and improvement

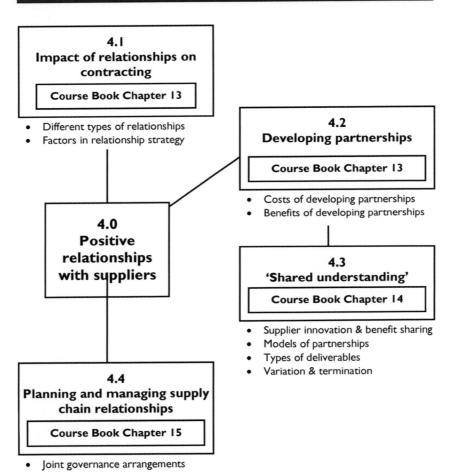

**4.1
Impact of relationships on contracting**

Course Book Chapter 13

- Different types of relationships
- Factors in relationship strategy

**4.2
Developing partnerships**

Course Book Chapter 13

- Costs of developing partnerships
- Benefits of developing partnerships

**4.0
Positive relationships with suppliers**

**4.3
'Shared understanding'**

Course Book Chapter 14

- Supplier innovation & benefit sharing
- Models of partnerships
- Types of deliverables
- Variation & termination

**4.4
Planning and managing supply chain relationships**

Course Book Chapter 15

- Joint governance arrangements
- Negotiation and problem-solving
- Market intelligence

Development of trust, info-sharing and co-operation > procurement efficiency, quality service delivery	Value for money, through collaborative cost reductions, continuous improvements etc

Management of supply risk

Benefits of positive supply relationships

Value for money through efficient arm's length sourcing

Potential for added value and synergy (2 + 2 = 5)

Return on relationship investment, by prioritising key relationships	Improved delivery of CSR/sustainability policy (by managing suppliers)

Types of supply relationship

 The **relationship spectrum** illustrates the range of relationships at various degrees of closeness or collaboration.

Competitive ↑

Relationship type	Characteristics
Adversarial relationship	Buyer and supplier are 'opponents', striving to obtain commercial advantage at the other's expense. Multi-sourcing and hard-negotiated short-term contracts for routine purchases.
Arm's length or transactional relationship	A distant, impersonal relationship: low-collaboration purchase of low-value, low-risk supplies; taking opportunistic advantage on price (eg e-auctions)
Preferred supplier relationship	Buyer grants regular business to a trusted supplier, on a preferential basis: eg by regular trading, call-off contracts or fixed contract.
Framework agreement	Buyer contracts with supplier(s) for a range of items, on agreed terms. User departments can then call off from suppliers as and when required.
Single sourcing	In relation to a particular item or range of items, the buyer grants exclusivity to a single supplier. Implies a high level of trust, mutual commitment and collaboration.
Partnership relationship	Buyer and supplier agree to collaborate closely for the long term on a range of issues, sharing information and ideas for development. Very high trust: aim is to find solutions that benefit both parties.

↓ *Collaborative*

Competitive relationships	Collaborative relationships
Buying organisation seeks to obtain the best price possible, at the expense of the supplier's profit margin (and *vice versa*).	Buying organisation seeks to develop long-term relationship with supplier: work together to add value, to mutual benefit.
No recognition of mutual interests: simple exchanges between buyer/seller.	Proactive joint search for improvements and innovations > share in benefits.
<ul><li>Distant (formal) communications</li><li>Win-lose approach to negotiations</li><li>Little trust, contact, info-sharing</li><li>Emphasis on single transactions, short-term contracts, tight controls</li></ul>	<ul><li>Joint search for efficiency, improvement</li><li>Agreed dovetailed objectives</li><li>Openness and transparency</li><li>Recognise need for exit strategy: no complacency</li></ul>

Benefits:	Benefits:
☑ Obtains value for buyer that would otherwise be retained by supplier ☑ Minimises costs of relationship development and management ☑ Cost efficient for routine, non-critical supplies with many suppliers and low switching costs	☑ Established points of contact > trust ☑ Awareness of capabilities/requirements > managed expectations, better service ☑ Sharing data/plans > forward planning ☑ Pooled expertise > quality, added value ☑ Reduced transaction costs

- *80:20 rule (Pareto principle):* invest in collaborative relationships with small number of important suppliers/items (eg using Kraljic matrix) + maintain competitive relationships to maximise value, minimise cost of routine/leverage items
- *Adversarial-collaborative relationships:* buyer works collaboratively with supplier at operational level to increase value – but competes commercially to appropriate as much of value as possible (eg in competitive tendering)
- *Innovative/constructive initiatives:* eg Building Schools for the Future (early supplier involvement and integration); ICT partnerships with central government departments (accelerating development/support for e-services).

Drivers for long-term, collaborative relationships:
❑ Growing trust, familiarity, rationalisation of supply base, mutual adaptation over time ❑ Recognition that whole supply chains create value – not just individual organisations ❑ Shorter product lifecycles > collaborative product development, responsive supply ❑ Trend to outsource non-core activities > collaboration/trust, to minimise risk ❑ ICT developments, supporting inter-organisational networks and relationships ❑ Sustainable procurement, reputation management etc > need for supply chain trust ❑ VFM pressure for 'lean' supply > need for collaboration to reduce wastes ❑ Costs of adversarial relationships: compliant (rather than committed performance), loss of preferential treatment, loss of potential synergy and improvements

Factors affecting relationship strategy

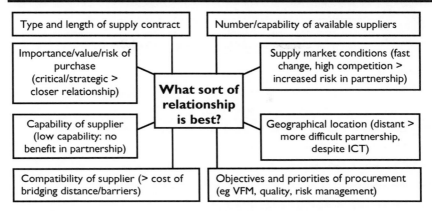

Strategic or operational requirement	*Strategic* (high value, long term, high risk, critical to policy): • Collaboration to develop complex solutions, manage risks etc • Mutual commitment to secure supply continuity • Development of trust to support info sharing *Operational* (low value, short term, low risk): • Need for competitive/arm's length approach to secure best price/value, minimise procurement costs
Clarity re requirement	Unclear/uncertain requirement: collaboration/trust to support flexibility, solution/specification development, testing, improvement
Competition in supply market	• Competitive market: transactional purchasing > exploit competing offers/prices, minimise relationship costs • Little competition > long-term relationship to maximise value, avoid switching costs, secure supply – *but* prevent complacency
Duration	• One-off/short-term contracts: solution/project-management focus, balance of technical/commercial considerations • Long-term contracts: need for collaboration, development of trust, flexibility, conflict resolution
Power of buyer/supplier	High power in relationship: can use competitive leverage, switching etc to secure best deal Low power: seek mutual commitment to minimise risk. Power imbalance: manage issues of trust, dependency, conflict

Partnership relationships

Partnership sourcing is a commitment by customers/suppliers, regardless of size, to a long-term relationship based on clear mutually agreed objectives to strive for world class capability and effectiveness. *(CBI, DTI)*

Requires:

- Top-level management commitment
- Involvement by all relevant disciplines/functions
- Customer and supplier working together for collective long-term advantage
- Spirit of openness and trust: sharing knowledge, business improvements and risk
- Clear joint objectives
- Proactive approach to improvement and developing the partnership
- Total quality management philosophy and flexibility

Beneficial where:

- ❑ Contracting body has high spend with supplier
- ❑ Contracting body faces high risk (continuity of supply vital)
- ❑ Requirement is technical/complex (high switching cost)
- ❑ Supplier relationship is 'high hassle' (due to importance/complexity of requirement)
- ❑ Product/service is new
- ❑ Supply market is fast-changing or restricted (closer links > expertise, secure supply)

Developing trust in buyer-supplier relationships

Contractual trust	>	Competence trust	>	Goodwill trust
Buyer and supplier can be relied on to do what they have agreed to do.		Supplier can be relied on to perform to specified standards.		Buyer and supplier believe in each other's integrity, dependability.
Based on track record of reliable compliance.		Based on skill, knowledge, process capability.		Based on mutual empathy and shared experience.
Basis for continuing relationship.		Basis for cost/time savings (eg reduced inspection)		Basis for increased info sharing and co-operation.

HOW are partnerships developed? **[>> Unit 4.3]**

Potential costs of developing partnership

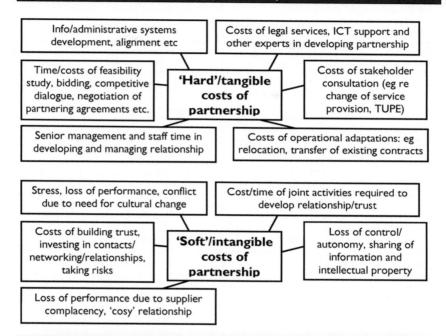

Info/administrative systems development, alignment etc

Costs of legal services, ICT support and other experts in developing partnership

Time/costs of feasibility study, bidding, competitive dialogue, negotiation of partnering agreements etc.

'Hard'/tangible costs of partnership

Costs of stakeholder consultation (eg re change of service provision, TUPE)

Senior management and staff time in developing and managing relationship

Costs of operational adaptations: eg relocation, transfer of existing contracts

Stress, loss of performance, conflict due to need for cultural change

Cost/time of joint activities required to develop relationship/trust

Costs of building trust, investing in contacts/networking/relationships, taking risks

'Soft'/intangible costs of partnership

Loss of control/autonomy, sharing of information and intellectual property

Loss of performance due to supplier complacency, 'cosy' relationship

Potential benefits of developing partnership

Improved communications	Integration of info/communication systems Established lines of communication, points of contact
Integrated systems	Systems integration for collaborative demand forecasting, planning, inventory management, project management etc.
Shared understanding of requirement	Opportunity to refine understanding of requirement over time; develop offering through continuous improvement; clear up ambiguities; understand one another's capabilities etc.
Improved problem solving/ dispute resolution	Established trust/goodwill + interpersonal communication channels + interest in win-win solutions + defined escalation and dispute resolution procedures >> motivation and mechanisms to resolve problems/disputes constructively
Continuous cost, quality and process improvements	Learning curve effects + integrated systems + collaboration on problem solving, waste reduction, continuous improvement + win-win benefits of improving efficiency/quality >> potential for collaborative ongoing improvements.

Overview: advantages and disadvantages of partnerships

Advantages for the buyer	Disadvantages for the buyer
Greater stability of supply and prices	Risk of complacency re cost/quality
Sharing of risk and investment	Less flexibility to change suppliers at need
Better supplier motivation	Possible risk to confidentiality
Cost savings from reduced supplier base, collaborative cost-reduction	May be locked into relationship with incompatible or inflexible supplier
Access to supplier technology/expertise	Restricted by EU procurement directives
Joint planning and info sharing > capacity management and efficiency	May be locked into relationship, despite supply market changes and opportunities
Ability to plan long-term improvements	Costs of relationship management
More influence with supplier	Possible loss of flexibility and control

Advantages for the supplier	Disadvantages for the supplier
Greater stability and volume of business, enabling investment in development	May be 'locked in' despite incompatible customer, market changes/opportunities
Working with customers > improved service, learning and development	Gains/risks may not be fairly shared in the partnership (depending on power balance)
Joint planning and info sharing > capacity management and efficiency	Risk of customer exploiting transparency (eg on costings, to force prices down)
Sharing of risk and investment	Cost of relationship management
Cost saving from efficiency, collaborative cost reduction, payment on time	Dependency on supplier may create loss of flexibility and control
Access customer technology/expertise	Restricted by EU procurement directives

Shared understanding

> **Shared understanding** is the ability of multiple agents to exploit common/ shared bodies of knowledge for the purposes of accomplishing common/ shared goals. It implies knowledge of the objectives, values, rules and protocols of a project or relationship, which guides collaborative activity.

- ☑ Provides shared, agreed-upon interpretation of contract terms, deliverables, expectations, protocols etc to guide collaborative action
- ☑ Enables co-ordination of effort without restrictive rules/instructions at every stage
- ☑ Minimises potential for misunderstanding, frustration and conflict
- ☑ Reduces time/cost of negotiations, meetings, reviews, conflict resolutions etc.
- ☑ Supports flexibility, innovation and synergy, by focusing on core values/deliverables: what desired level of performance/relationship 'looks like'
- ☑ Regarded as essential to the success of partnerships, collaborations and 'coalition' operations (eg complex supply projects)

Supplier innovation

> **Innovation** is 'the successful exploitation of new ideas'. Supplier innovation implies investment by suppliers in problem-solving and innovation to meet requirements in new ways (or to meet new requirements).

- ☑ Innovative solutions offer added-value or cost-saving solutions to requirement
- ☑ Innovative solutions often required to newly emerging problems eg 'green'
- ☑ Increasing demand for innovative solutions supports further innovation

Innovation involves investment, experimentation, risk and flexibility. Requires:

- Shared understanding re expectations/objectives (often loosely defined to begin with)
- Shared understanding re cost/risk/benefit sharing
- Risk management: eg trialling/piloting or phase-gate (staged) project management
- Evidence of successful innovation: activities and outcomes

Contracting bodies can support supplier innovation by:

- Sourcing innovative products, services and processes (including new ways of thinking about procurement), as they become available and viable options
- Selecting, supporting and leveraging the capabilities of suppliers who are innovating
- Supporting networking and collaboration to develop best-practice supply solutions

> **Forward Commitment Procurement (FCP)** is 'a commitment to purchase, at a point in the future, a product that does not yet exist commercially, against a specification that current products do not meet at a sufficient scale, to make it worthwhile for suppliers to invest in tooling up and manufacture' (*Sustainable Procurement Task Force*)

Benefit sharing

Shared understanding re supplier share of benefits from investment in innovation eg:

- ☑ Retained ownership of intellectual property rights in designs/processes
- ☑ Potential to offer developed solutions/capabilities to other customers/clients
- ☑ Long contract, options to renew, guaranteed volume business
- ☑ Other gain-sharing and incentive arrangements   *[>> Unit 2.6]*

Developing partnership   *(Partnership Sourcing Initiative)*

Which markets? Which products/services?

↓

Sell the idea (to management, stakeholders, potential partners)

↓

Choose your partners (using defined criteria)

↓

Define desired outcomes
(style, methods, continuous improvement, exit strategy)

↓

Make partnering relationship work

Developing partnership   *(Ellram)*

1. Assessment: scope/nature/duration of contract; common vision of future; clearly defined goals; recognition of resource requirement; acceptance of need to change

↓

2. Preparing: all tender docs stressing partnering; recognition of need for due diligence; plan for consultation/training; project plans; establishment of budget

↓

3. Framing issues: risk apportionment; length/scope of contract; governance issues; terms of charter; incentives; ownership of IP; change controls; exit strategies

↓

4. Making collaborative decisions: working through negotiation/competitive dialogue co-operatively; establishing governance framework (partnership board)

↓

5. Maintaining relationship: contract management; consultation; blame-free problem-solving; reporting success; achieving improvements; meeting commitments

Deliverables, targets and deadlines

Contract and partnership agreement/charter must promote shared understanding of *measurable output/outcomes* from project/relationship: 'deliverables'.

❑ Delivery to site of goods in satisfactory condition at required time (basic supply)
❑ Performance of required service to standard set out in specification and service level agreement (services)
❑ Agreed levels of investment in the provision of services (eg outsourcing contracts)
❑ Report (eg consultancy/research contract)
❑ Time-phased deliverables at project milestones (eg construction)
❑ Specified levels of improvement, cost reduction, sustainability gains etc

Shared understanding also required re:

❑ Timescales/deadlines and targets/KPIs defining satisfactory performance
❑ Consequences of non-performance (eg liquidated damages or service credits)
❑ Responsibilities and mechanisms for monitoring and reporting progress/performance

Variation and change control

❑ Contract clause stipulating express agreement in writing on any variation in terms

❑ Pre-agreed circumstances in which variations can be made

❑ Contract managers responsible for agreeing/implementing variations:
  • Consulting stakeholders
  • Checking financial, budgetary, operational and service implications
  • Agreeing charges for variations with supplier
  • Issuing submission to budget holder for approval
  • Amending the contract (with audit trail)
  • Notifying supplier and affected stakeholders.

Exit strategies

Shared understanding required re factors triggering termination, procedures for exit.

❑ Termination clause in contract, defining rules/standards and reasons for termination, notice periods, liability etc. Clauses may specifically cover termination due to supplier default, supplier liquidation, persistent breach, *force majeure,* change of ownership.

❑ Procedures for pursuing grievances/disputes: escalation, conciliation, arbitration etc

❑ Exit/transition clause covering service transfer: guaranteeing co-operative approach to handover, provision of information etc

❑ Separate schedule (referred to in exit clause): detailed operational requirements for transfer of services. Eg: roles in managing exit plan; timescales for exit; disposal of physical assets and intellectual property; staff transfer (TUPE) issues; resource requirements; how transfer (novation) of contract will take place; due diligence plan.

Tools of relationship management

Relationship charters	Drawn up at the outset of a partnership arrangement by senior policy makers, to achieve shared understanding [>> Unit 4.3] ❑ Scope of engagement ❑ Roles, responsibilities and ownership of tasks ❑ Benchmarks for behaviour ❑ Performance measurement and agreed KPIs/deliverables ❑ Communication channels and methods ❑ Monitoring, review and evaluation schedule and methods
Relationship management principles	❑ Delivery of mutual KPIs, expectations and contract terms ❑ Equitable sharing of risks and benefits/gains ❑ Communication (at level appropriate to relationship) ❑ Joint approach to managing and improving performance of the contract > future mutually beneficial outcomes ❑ Constructive, proactive approach to problem solving
Joint governance arrangements	❑ Appropriate to strategic/operational nature of relationships ❑ Mechanisms for decision-making, reporting, collaboration ❑ Tiered structure for governance at appropriate levels, empowered to make decisions within terms of reference (reducing length of channels, bureaucratic processes) **Eg** *Siemens Business Services and National Savings & Investment* contract for outsourcing of operations: ❑ Top level: formulation of agreements, policy-making, review ❑ Partnership Development Board: strategic vision/direction ❑ Executive Boards: periodic meetings with standing agenda ❑ Middle/lower level (eg Management Groups, supported by Cross Business Teams, Work Groups) reporting on implementation and performance against targets
Strategic relationship strategies	❑ Supplier relationship management ❑ Collaborative planning, forecasting and replenishment ❑ Partnership sourcing ❑ Supplier development ❑ Supply chain management